Content

Chicken Florentine Style

A creamy, elegant dish featuring tender chicken breasts served with a rich spinach sauce. An ideal choice for making a statement on a special occasion or an unforgettable date night.

Sheet Pan Chicken Shawarma

This Middle Eastern favorite is easy to prepare on a single sheet pan, full of flavors like cumin, coriander, and garlic. Serve with pita, hummus, and a salad.

Chicken Katsu

A Japanese crispy fried chicken cutlet served with tangy katsu sauce. Great as a main course or in sandwiches.

Chicken Adobo

The famous Filipino dish where chicken is simmered in a flavorful mixture of soy sauce, vinegar, garlic, and bay leaves.

Chicken Stir-Fry

A quick and healthy stir-fry recipe packed with vibrant vegetables and a savory sauce. Great for a busy weeknight.

One-Pan Chicken and Rice with Preserved Lemon

A Moroccan-inspired dish where chicken is baked with fragrant spices, rice, and tangy preserved lemon.

Chicken Yakitori and Rice

Japanese-style grilled chicken skewers glazed with a savory sauce, served over steamed rice.

Caramel Chicken

A Vietnamese dish that blends sweet and savory flavors by cooking chicken in a caramelized fish sauce.

Chicken Fajita Salad

A fresh and flavorful salad with grilled chicken, bell peppers, and onions, topped with a zesty lime dressing.

Chicken Meatball Casserole

Tender chicken meatballs baked in a cheesy, tomato-based casserole for a comforting meal the whole family will love.

Chicken Spaghetti

A creamy pasta dish loaded with chicken, cheese, and a flavorful tomato sauce. Comfort food at its finest.

Butter Chicken

A simplified version of the classic Indian butter chicken, with a creamy tomato-based sauce. Serve with naan or rice for a cozy meal.

Pan-Seared Chicken with Pear Slaw

Juicy pan-seared chicken breasts served with a refreshing and crunchy pear slaw for a perfect balance of flavors.

Butter Grilled Wings Recipe

Crispy, grilled chicken wings tossed in a delicious butter sauce. Great for game day or a laid-back get-together.

Chicken Teriyaki

Japanese-style grilled chicken with a glossy, savory-sweet teriyaki sauce. Simple and satisfying.

Three Cup Chicken Recipe

A Taiwanese dish cooked with soy sauce, rice wine, and sesame oil for a flavorful punch.

Spicy Labneh Fried Chicken Sandwich Recipe

Crispy fried chicken paired with a spicy, tangy labneh spread on a soft bun for the ultimate sandwich experience.

Chicken Enchiladas

Rolled tortillas filled with tender chicken and cheese, topped with a flavorful enchilada sauce and baked to perfection.

Slow Cooker Chicken Tinga

A slow-cooked Mexican dish with shredded chicken simmered in a smoky, tomato-based sauce. Perfect as a topping for tacos, burritos, or enjoyed by itself.

Chicken Strips Recipe

Classic crispy chicken strips, seasoned and breaded to perfection. Ideal for dipping in your favorite sauce.

Chicken Florentine Style

Ingredients

4 boneless skinless chicken breasts
Salt and freshly ground black pepper
All-purpose flour, for dredging
6 tablespoons (3/4 stick) unsalted butter
2 tablespoons shallots, sliced
1 tablespoon chopped garlic
1 1/2 cups dry white wine
1 cup whipping cream
1 tablespoon chopped fresh Italian parsley
20 ounces of thawed and drained frozen spinach

How to Make

Add a little pepper and salt to the chicken.

Lightly coat the chicken with flour by dredging it in it.

Toss away any extra flour.

Two tablespoons of butter should be melted over medium heat in a heavy, big skillet.

Pan-fry the chicken for 5 minutes per side until browned.

To keep the chicken warm, move it to a platter and cover it with foil.

In the same pan, melt two tablespoons of butter over medium heat.

Add the garlic and shallots, and sauté for one minute, turning to scrape up any browned pieces on the bottom of the skillet, or until the shallots are transparent.

Pour in the wine

Raise the heat to medium-high and boil for approximately three minutes, or until the liquid has reduced by half.

After adding the cream, simmer the sauce for three minutes, stirring often, or until it reduces by half.

Add the parsley and stir.

Add salt and pepper to taste when preparing the sauce.

Turn the chicken to coat it in the sauce after adding it to the sauce along with any collected juices.

Meanwhile, heat another large skillet over medium heat to melt the remaining 2 tablespoons of butter.

When the spinach is fully cooked, add it and sauté it.

Add salt and pepper to taste while seasoning the spinach.

Spread out the spinach on a serving dish.

Top the spinach with the chicken. After adding the sauce, serve.

Sheet Pan Chicken Shawarma

Ingredients

2 tablespoons olive oil
1 teaspoon ground cumin
1/2 teaspoon ground cinnamon
1/4 teaspoon ground allspice
1/4 teaspoon ground cardamom
1/4 teaspoon ground turmeric
2 cloves garlic, grated
Kosher salt and freshly ground black pepper

1 pound sliced chicken thighs
1 medium onion, sliced
1/2 cup full-fat Greek yogurt
Juice of 1/2 lemon
4 pieces pita bread
3 dill pickle spears, chopped
1 Roma tomato (about 6 ounces), chopped
1 cup shredded lettuce

How to Make

Preheat the oven to 450 degrees F.
Mix the olive oil, spices, salt, and pepper in a bowl.
Add the chicken and onions, and toss to coat.
Spread them on a sheet pan in a single layer.
Bake for about 15 minutes until the chicken is done and the onions are
lightly browned.
Stir the yogurt, lemon juice, and pepper until smooth.
Warm the pitas in the microwave on a microwave-safe plate, 30 seconds
to 1 minute.

Spread the yogurt sauce over the pitas and add the chicken and onions
on top.
Top with the pickles, tomatoes and shredded lettuce.

Chicken Katsu

Ingredients

For Katsu Sauce:
1/2 cup ketchup
3 tablespoons Worcestershire sauce
2 tablespoons low-sodium soy sauce

For Chicken:
1/4 cup all-purpose flour
2 large eggs, lightly beaten
1 1/2 cups panko
Kosher salt and freshly ground black pepper
2 boneless skinless chicken breasts, butterflied and cut into 4 cutlets
1 1/2 cups vegetable or canola oil
2 cups finely sliced cabbage
Cooked white rice, for serving
4 lemon wedges

How to Make

Mix the ketchup, Worcestershire sauce, and soy sauce in a small bowl and set it aside.

For the chicken: Prepare a wire rack on a baking sheet or line a large plate with paper towels.
Arrange the flour, eggs, and panko in separate shallow dishes.
Mix 1 teaspoon salt and 1 teaspoon pepper and season both sides of the cutlets with this mixture.
For each cutlet, coat it in flour, then dip it in eggs, and finally cover it with panko, pressing gently to ensure it sticks.
Place the coated cutlet on a plate and repeat with the rest.

Preheat the oil in a large skillet over high heat until it reaches around 350 degrees F on a deep-fry thermometer.
To check if it's ready, drop a few pieces of panko into the oil.
It should bubble vigorously.

Cook the chicken cutlets in batches, searing each side until golden brown, about 3 minutes per side, to avoid overcrowding.
Transfer to the prepared wire rack or plate, season with salt and let rest for 2 minutes.
Meanwhile, repeat with the remaining 2 cutlets.

Slice each cutlet crosswise into 1/2-inch strips, lay on a bed of sliced cabbage and serve with the katsu sauce, rice and a lemon wedge.

Chicken Adobo

Ingredients

2/3 cup apple cider vinegar
1/4 cup soy sauce
2 tablespoons light brown sugar
1 teaspoon whole black peppercorns
Large pinch crushed red pepper
4 garlic cloves, crushed
2 bay leaves
8 chicken drumsticks
1 scallion, thinly sliced
Cooked rice, for serving

How to Make

In a large resealable plastic bag, add vinegar, soy sauce, sugar, peppercorns, red pepper flakes, garlic, bay leaves, and 1/2 cup of water. Seal the bag tightly and shake it well to mix the ingredients thoroughly and ensure the sugar is dissolved.
Place the chicken in the bag, seal it, and gently shake to evenly coat the chicken with the marinade.
Transfer the bag to the refrigerator and allow it to marinate for a minimum of 2 hours, or leave it overnight for enhanced flavor.
Place an oven rack in the highest position and set the oven to preheat using the broiler function.

Transfer the contents of the bag into a large Dutch oven or pot, spreading the chicken evenly in a single layer.
Heat over high until it reaches a boil, then cover the pot.
Lower the heat to a simmer and cook the chicken, turning the drumsticks occasionally.
Continue cooking until the chicken becomes tender and reaches an internal temperature of 165°F at the thickest part of the leg, about 25 to 30 minutes.
Raise the heat to high and bring the remaining liquid in the pot to a rolling boil.
Let it cook until it reduces to a consistency slightly thinner than maple syrup, about 7 to 9 minutes.
Strain the sauce to remove the solids, discarding them afterward.

While the sauce simmers, broil the chicken until golden and slightly charred in areas, flipping halfway through, about 3 to 4 minutes on each side. Once cooked, place the chicken in a shallow dish and generously drizzle the sauce on top.
Garnish with fresh scallions and serve alongside rice.
tomatoes and shredded lettuce.

Chicken Stir-Fry

Ingredients

One 12-ounce portion of boneless, skinless chicken breast, perfect for lean protein in a variety of dishes.

2 tablespoons light soy sauce

1 tablespoon plus 2 teaspoons cornstarch

3 tablespoons vegetable oil

One 1-inch piece ginger, peeled and cut into matchsticks

2 cloves garlic, chopped

8 ounces broccoli florets

4 ounces of shiitake or button mushrooms, with stems removed and sliced into 1/2 inch thick pieces.

One small carrot, peeled and sliced into thin, 3-inch-long strips.

1 tablespoon Shaoxing wine

1/2 cup low-sodium chicken stock

1/4 teaspoon ground white pepper, optional

1 teaspoon toasted sesame oil

3 cups steamed jasmine rice, for serving

How to Make

Chill the chicken breast in the freezer for roughly 20 minutes, or until it becomes firm enough to slice thinly.
Using a sharp or serrated knife, thinly slice the chicken 1/8 inch thick.
Pour into a medium bowl and gently mix in 1 tablespoon of soy sauce. Let sit for 10 minutes.
Combine 1 tablespoon of vegetable oil with 1 tablespoon of cornstarch, stirring thoroughly to blend.
Allow the mixture to rest in a cool location for 20 minutes.
Whisk the remaining 2 teaspoons of cornstarch with 2 teaspoons water in a small bowl; set aside.

Heat the remaining 2 tablespoons of vegetable oil in a wok or large nonstick skillet over medium-high heat.
Once the oil is hot and shimmering, arrange the chicken slices in a single, even layer in the pan.
Let them cook undisturbed until they begin to turn opaque, approximately 45 seconds.
Flip the chicken and continue to cook undisturbed until the pieces are mostly opaque, for another 45 seconds to 1 minute. Remove to a bowl.

Add the ginger and garlic to the wok.
Cook, stirring frequently, until the garlic turns a light golden brown, approximately 30 seconds.
Add the broccoli and toss to coat; cook, stirring occasionally, for 1 minute.

Add the mushrooms and carrot; toss to combine.

Pour in the Shaoxing wine and continue cooking, making sure to deglaze the pan by scraping up all the caramelized bits stuck to the bottom.

Add the chicken stock, white pepper if using, chicken and the remaining 1 tablespoon soy sauce.

Combine the cornstarch mixture thoroughly in the bowl, then pour it into the wok.

Stir well to coat all the ingredients, then lower the heat to medium-low and cover with a lid.

Allow the sauce to thicken and the chicken to cook completely, which should take about 2 minutes.

Drizzle with the sesame oil. Mix thoroughly until everything is evenly combined, then transfer to a serving platter.

Serve warm alongside a side of steamed rice for a complete and satisfying meal.

One-Pan Chicken and Rice with Preserved Lemon

Ingredients

1 1/2 cups basmati rice

1 teaspoon ground cumin

1 teaspoon ground coriander

1 teaspoon paprika

1/2 teaspoon ground cinnamon

1/2 teaspoon ground turmeric

Kosher salt

Four tender, boneless, and skinless chicken breasts, each weighing between 6 to 8 ounces.

4 tablespoons extra-virgin olive oil

1 large onion, chopped

3 cloves garlic, minced

1 preserved lemon

3/4 cup pitted green olives

1 1/2 cups chicken broth

1/2 cup parsley leaves, chopped

How to Make

Rinse the rice 3 to 5 times, allowing it to drain each time, to remove any excess starch and ensure a fluffier texture.
Set aside.

In a small bowl, mix together cumin, coriander, paprika, cinnamon, turmeric, and 1 teaspoon of salt.
Use paper towels to pat the chicken breasts dry, then coat both sides with half of the spice blend.

Heat 2 tablespoons of oil in a large (12-inch) pan or cast-iron skillet over medium heat.
Once the oil is shimmering (but not smoking), add the chicken.
Sear each side until it develops a rich, golden brown crust, about 3 to 5 minutes per side.
Remove the chicken and set aside.

Add the remaining 2 tablespoons of oil to the same pan and heat over medium.
Sauté the onion, stirring occasionally, until it turns golden brown, approximately 5 minutes.
Add the garlic and sauté for another minute, allowing the flavors to meld and the garlic to become fragrant.
Mix in the rice along with the leftover spice blend, stirring thoroughly to combine all the ingredients.

Remove the flesh of the preserved lemon (discard the seeds and save the flesh for another use).
Finely chop the lemon rind (peel).
Stir in the rind with the rice, then incorporate the olives for added flavor.
Add the broth and 1 1/2 cups of water to the pan, then raise the heat to medium-high.
Bring to a simmer, place the chicken breasts back in the pan and cover the pan.
Lower the heat to medium and simmer until the rice is soft and the chicken is fully cooked, approximately 30 minutes

A staple of Arab Mediterranean cuisines, preserved lemons can be found at specialty stores or online or made at home a few weeks in advance.
If the rice is still firm after 30 minutes, add 1/4 cup water and cook for another 10 minutes.

Serve the chicken whole for a hearty presentation, or shred it and mix it back into the rice for a more integrated flavor.
Serve sprinkled with parsley.

Chicken Yakitori and Rice

Ingredients

2 cups chicken stock

1 cup white rice

Salt

About 3 tablespoons neutral oil

About 1/2 cup dark soy or tamari

1/4 cup mirin

1/4 cup sake

2 tablespoons brown sugar

4 large cloves of peeled garlic

1-inch ginger root

2 pounds of boneless, skinless chicken thighs

1 bunch large scallions, trimmed

Green Beans with Tofu and Sesame Sauce

For Green Beans with Tofu and Sesame Sauce
Ingredients

1 pound trimmed green beans (two 8-ounce packages or trim
1 pound fresh green beans the day you shop)
4 tablespoons toasted sesame seeds
Use approximately 1 tablespoon of soy sauce (choose dark
soy sauce or tamari for a savory kick) to enhance the flavor
of green beans. Alternatively, for a sweeter, milder touch,
consider substituting with mirin or sake.
1 round teaspoon sugar or fine sugar
4 ounces firm tofu

How to Make

For the chicken yakitori and rice: Before grilling, immerse the
skewers in water to prevent them from burning.
Gather ingredients.

In a saucepan, bring 2 cups of chicken stock or broth to a boil.
Stir in white rice and a small pinch of salt.
Once boiling, reduce the heat to low, cover the pan, and simmer for
15 to 18 minutes until the rice is tender and has absorbed the liquid.
Fluff and leave pot covered.

Preheat a sizable cast-iron or nonstick skillet over medium-high to
high heat, adding a generous amount of oil—enough to coat the
bottom of the pan with three full turns.
Meanwhile, to a small pot add soy sauce or tamari, mirin, sake,
brown sugar, grated garlic and grated ginger.

Heat the mixture until it reaches a gentle boil and thickens, stirring for a few minutes.
Remove from heat and set aside about one-third of the mixture for serving. Place a basting brush into the pot with the remaining sauce.

Meanwhile, cut the chicken and scallions into bite-sized pieces.
Drain skewers and thread on chicken and scallions, packed firmly.

Cook the skewers in a pan for 8 to 10 minutes, turning them occasionally.
After the chicken and onions have browned on the first side, baste them with sauce as you turn them.
If the pan starts to smoke excessively, lower the heat slightly.

Enjoy skewers served over a bed of fluffy white rice, accompanied by crisp green beans on the side.

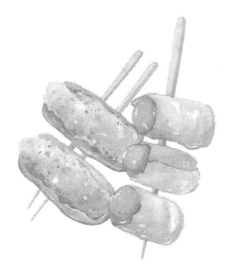

How to Make Green Beans with Tofu and Sesame Sauce:
Gather ingredients.

Heat a few inches of water in a deep skillet until it reaches a rolling boil.
Cut green beans into thirds.

Place toasted sesame seeds into a mortar and pestle.
Add a splash of soy sauce, mirin, or sake, and a pinch of sugar. Gently grind and mix until the ingredients are well combined, creating a flavorful blend.
Grind into paste (but some whole sesame seeds are fine), 2 minutes.

Blanch green beans in boiling water for approximately 4 minutes until they reach a tender-crisp texture.
If you're not using soy sauce, consider adding a pinch of salt to the water for enhanced flavor.
Drain in strainer and run under cool water 1 minute; drain off excess water by leaving in strainer a few minutes.

Crumble about 4 ounces of the tofu with fingertips. Lightly toss crispy tofu cubes and fresh green beans in a nutty sesame sauce for a deliciously satisfying dish.
Serve warm for a flavorful, protein-packed meal that's both nourishing and easy to prepare.

Caramel Chicken

Ingredients

2 tablespoons unsalted butter
1/2 cup dark brown sugar
8 cloves garlic, finely minced
One 2-inch piece ginger, finely minced
1/3 cup rice vinegar
1/4 cup fish sauce
1/4 cup low-sodium soy sauce
8 skin-on, bone-in chicken thighs
Kosher salt and freshly ground black pepper
1 tablespoon coconut or vegetable oil
White rice, for serving

How to Make

Preheat the oven to 400 degrees F.

Melt the butter in a small saucepan over medium-high heat.
Add the brown sugar and cook, stirring constantly, until it begins to melt, 2 to 3 minutes.
Add the garlic and ginger and cook, continuing to stir, for another 1 to 2 minutes.
Stir in the vinegar, fish sauce and soy sauce.
Bring to a low simmer and let cook for about 5 minutes.
Remove from the heat.

Use a paper towel to thoroughly pat dry the chicken. Sprinkle both sides with salt and pepper.

Heat a large ovenproof skillet over high heat until very hot.
Add the oil.
Place the chicken in the skillet skin-side down and let brown without moving it for about 4 minutes.
Remove the chicken to a plate and raise the heat to medium-high.
Add the brown sugar mixture and use a wooden spoon to scrape up any browned bits.
Return the chicken to the skillet skin-side up.
Transfer the skillet to the oven and bake, basting the chicken with the sauce midway through cooking, until cooked through, about 20 minutes.
For extra-crispy skin, transfer the skillet to the broiler for about 2 minutes.
Serve over white rice with sauce.

Chicken Fajita Salad

Ingredients

For Fajita Mix:

1 tablespoon chili powder
1 tablespoon ground cumin
1 teaspoon garlic powder
1 teaspoon granulated sugar
1 teaspoon kosher salt
1/2 teaspoon red pepper flakes
1/2 teaspoon freshly ground black pepper

For Salad:

4 tablespoons of olive oil, with additional oil reserved for greasing the grill.
6 boneless, skinless chicken breasts
2 red bell peppers, quartered
2 yellow bell peppers, quartered
3 ears corn, silks and husks removed, halved crosswise
3 avocados, halved and pitted
1/2 lime, for squeezing

For Cilantro Lime Dressing:

1/2 cup olive oil
2 tablespoons fresh cilantro,
chopped
1 teaspoon lime zest plus 1/4 cup
lime juice
1 teaspoon kosher salt
1/2 teaspoon chili flakes

For Assembly:

1 head romaine lettuce, leaves
separated
1 head butter lettuce, leaves
separated
1 bunch fresh cilantro sprigs,
whole
1 pint grape tomatoes, halved
lengthwise
4 limes, halved crosswise
One wheel of Cotija cheese,
crumbled into sizable chunks,
perfect for adding a bold,
tangy flavor to your dishes.

How to Make

To prepare the fajita seasoning:

Combine chili powder, cumin, garlic powder, sugar, salt,
red pepper flakes, and black pepper in a mixing bowl and
stir until well blended.
Combine the chili powder, cumin, garlic powder, sugar,
salt, red pepper flakes, and black pepper in a bowl,
mixing thoroughly to ensure all the spices are evenly
distributed.

For the salad:
Preheat a grill or grill pan to medium-high and lightly coat it with olive oil.

Season the chicken breasts by spreading a third of the fajita mix on one side. Place the chicken, seasoned-side down, onto the grill. Then, evenly coat the top of the chicken with the remaining third of the fajita mix. Grill the chicken until cooked through, about 5 minutes per side; this will depend on the size of the breasts. Remove the chicken to a baking sheet to cool.

Once the chicken has cooled, pour 2 tablespoons of olive oil into a large mixing bowl, then add the remaining fajita seasoning.

Whisk everything together until well combined.

Add the peppers and toss to coat.

Grill the peppers, turning occasionally to achieve even grill marks, for approximately 3 minutes per side.

Once done, transfer them to a baking sheet to cool.

Brush the corn with the last 2 tablespoons olive oil. Place the corn on the grill, turning occasionally, and cook for about 10 minutes or until the kernels are tender and have a nice golden-brown char.

Remove to a plate to cool.

Cut the chicken into crosswise slices, ensuring the slices remain attached. Do the same with the avocado, slicing it crosswise while keeping the slices in place. Drizzle a bit of lime juice over the avocado to keep it from turning brown.

For the assembly: Arrange the lettuce leaves on a large board or platter. Arrange the chicken breast slices, avocado slices, and peppers evenly over the bed of leaves. Scatter the corn cobs throughout and add sprigs of cilantro in various spots for a burst of fresh flavor. It should look more free-form than composed. Next, incorporate the tomatoes, lime halves, and cheese chunks, arranging them similarly. Drizzle a bit of dressing over the salad to give it a hint of flavor and serve the rest on the side.

Chicken Meatball Casserole

Ingredients

For Meatballs:
Nonstick Cooking Spray (Ensure your baked goods and meals come out effortlessly with our Nonstick Cooking Spray. Perfect for coating baking sheets and dishes, this spray prevents sticking and makes clean-up a breeze.)

1 pound ground chicken

1/2 cup canned pumpkin

1/3 cup grated Parmesan

1/4 cup grated yellow onion

2 tablespoons minced fresh parsley

1 teaspoon kosher salt

1/2 teaspoon freshly ground black pepper

2 cloves garlic, minced

For Casserole:
Kosher salt

16-ounce box of mezzi rigatoni or mezze penne. (Perfectly designed for capturing rich sauces and providing a satisfying bite, this pasta is ideal for a variety of dishes from classic Italian pasta bakes to savory, sauce-coated meals. Made from high-quality durum wheat, it delivers both flavor and a delightful al dente consistency in every serving.)

One 24-ounce jar marinara sauce

2 cups shredded mozzarella

1/4 cup finely grated Parmesan cheese, with extra for sprinkling on top before serving.

How to Make

For the meatballs:
Preheat the oven to 350 degrees F.
Lightly coat a baking sheet with nonstick cooking spray to ensure your baked goods don't stick and come out easily.

Mix together the chicken, pumpkin, Parmesan, onion, parsley, salt, pepper and garlic in a large bowl.
Cover and refrigerate 20 minutes.

Using a tablespoon, form the mixture into balls and arrange them on the prepared baking sheet.
Bake for 12 to 15 minutes, or until fully cooked.
Next, raise the oven temperature to 400°F and lightly coat a 9-by-13-inch baking dish with cooking spray.

For the casserole:
Meanwhile, bring a large pot of water to a boil.
Season generously with salt.
Cook the pasta for 3 minutes shorter than the time indicated on the package.
Before draining, set aside 1/3 cup of the pasta cooking water, then drain the pasta.

Toss the pasta with the marinara sauce and pasta water in a large bowl. Transfer to the greased baking dish.
Nestle the meatballs into the pasta. Top with the mozzarella and sprinkle with the Parmesan.

Bake until the cheese turns a rich golden brown and becomes bubbly, which should take around 20 minutes. Let stand for 5 minutes. Serve with grated Parmesan.

Chicken Spaghetti

Ingredients

A whole raw chicken, expertly butchered into 8 distinct
pieces
One pound of delicate thin spaghetti, conveniently pre-
broken into 2-inch segments for easy cooking and
serving
2 1/2 cups shredded sharp Cheddar
1/4 cup finely diced green bell pepper
1/4 cup finely diced red bell pepper
1 teaspoon seasoned salt
1/8 to 1/4 teaspoon cayenne pepper
Two 10 3/4-ounce cans cream of mushroom soup
1 medium onion, finely diced
Salt and freshly ground black pepper

How to Make

Preheat the oven to 350 degrees F.

In a spacious pot, heat water until it reaches a vigorous boil with continuous bubbling. Once boiling, carefully add the chicken pieces and cook for a few minutes. Reduce the heat to medium-low and let the chicken simmer gently for 30 to 45 minutes, until fully cooked and tender.

Remove the chicken and 2 cups of the chicken cooking broth from the pot. Once the chicken has cooled, peel off the skin and shred the meat, combining both dark and white parts, to yield approximately 2 generous cups of shredded chicken.

Cook the spaghetti in the same chicken broth until it reaches an al dente texture. Do not overcook. When the spaghetti is cooked, combine with the chicken, mushroom soup, 1 1/2 cups cheese, the green peppers, red peppers, onions, seasoned salt, cayenne, and sprinkle with salt and pepper. Pour in 1 cup of the reserved chicken broth, and add up to another cup if necessary to achieve the desired consistency.

Transfer the mixture into a casserole dish and sprinkle the remaining 1 cup of cheese on top. You can either cover and freeze the casserole for up to 6 months, refrigerate it for up to 2 days, or bake it right away. To bake, cook until bubbly, which should take around 45 minutes. If the cheese starts to over-brown, simply cover the dish with foil.

Butter Chicken

Ingredients

For Marinade:

1/2 cup Greek yogurt
1 tablespoon chili powder
1 tablespoon ground cumin
1 tablespoon turmeric
1 tablespoon garam masala
1 tablespoon hot Hungarian paprika
Kosher salt and freshly ground black pepper
Two pounds of tender, boneless, skinless chicken strips, cut into convenient 1-inch pieces
4 tablespoons salted butter

Sauce:

1 cup crushed tomatoes
1 teaspoon sugar
2 frozen ginger pods (or equivalent to 2 inches of fresh ginger, finely grated)
2 frozen garlic pods (or 2 cloves garlic, grated)
Use 3/4 to 1 cup of heavy cream, brought to room temperature (This will ensure that the cream blends smoothly and evenly, enhancing the flavor and consistency of your dish)
Kosher salt and freshly ground black pepper

Serving:
1/4 cup finely chopped fresh cilantro, with extra for garnish
2 cups cooked basmati rice

How to Make

Marinade:
In a mixing bowl, combine the yogurt with chili powder, cumin, turmeric, garam masala, paprika, 2 teaspoons of salt, and a few cracks of black pepper. Stir well to blend the spices evenly into the yogurt. Stir until everything is one color. Transfer the mixture into a spacious resealable bag and then add the chicken pieces. Leave on the counter at room temperature for 2 hours.

To cook the chicken:
Heat a large pan with straight sides over medium-high heat and melt the butter. Once the butter is hot, add the chicken chunks from the bag, ensuring you discard the marinade before adding them to the pan. Cook, turning, until some parts are browned but most are still white, about 8 minutes.

For the sauce :
Stir in the crushed tomatoes, sugar, ginger, and garlic into the pan. Things should be bubbly and hot. Combine all ingredients and cook until the pan releases the aroma of garlic and ginger. Then, pour in the heavy cream, stirring continuously until the mixture is evenly blended and has a uniform color. Partially cover and simmer on low for 20 minutes.

For serving:
Add a handful of cilantro to the dish and mix well. Serve it over a bed of rice, garnished with an extra sprinkle of fresh cilantro for a burst of flavor.

Pan-Seared Chicken with Pear Slaw

Ingredients

2 tablespoons canola oil

Four generously sized, skin-on chicken breasts, each weighing between 5 to 6 ounces

Kosher salt and freshly ground black pepper

1/4 cup extra-virgin olive oil

1/2 cup rice wine vinegar

1 tablespoon sugar

1/2 teaspoon cumin seeds

1/2 teaspoon coriander seeds, lightly crushed

1 large clove garlic, grated

Three medium under ripe Anjou pears, peeled and sliced into thin matchstick strips (offering a crisp and subtly tart flavor)

4 stalks of celery, trimmed and sliced into delicate half-moons.

How to Make

Brown the Chicken:
Heat a large skillet over medium-high heat and pour in the canola oil.
Arrange the chicken pieces in a single layer on a tray, then season with salt and pepper.
Once the oil shimmers and begins to lightly smoke, use metal tongs to gently place the chicken pieces, skin-side down, into the hot oil.
Do not overcrowd the skillet. Cook the chicken by searing it and turning it every 2 to 3 minutes until it's nicely browned and reaches an internal temperature of 165°F.
This task is expected to be completed in about 10 to 12 minutes.

Make the dressing:
Prepare the dressing by combining olive oil, rice wine vinegar, sugar, cumin, coriander, and garlic in a large bowl.
Whisk the ingredients together thoroughly, adding a hearty pinch of salt to enhance the flavors.

Prepare the slaw:
Gently fold the pears and celery into the dressing, making sure they are evenly coated.
Refrigerate until you're ready to serve.

Serve:
Arrange the chicken breasts on a platter (or individual plates) and top with the slaw.

Butter Grilled Wings

Ingredients

For the chicken:

3 pounds chicken wings,
preferably party wings
2 teaspoons baking powder
2 teaspoons cornstarch
1 teaspoon kosher salt

For the sauce and serving:

2 cloves garlic
1 (1-inch) piece ginger
2 tablespoons unsalted butter
1/4 cup honey
2 tablespoons gochujang
(Korean chili paste)
2 tablespoons soy sauce or
tamari
1 tablespoon plus 1 1/2
teaspoons rice vinegar
1 teaspoon toasted sesame oil
1 medium scallion, thinly sliced
(optional)
White sesame seeds, for garnish
(optional)

How to Make

Make the wings:
Preheat your outdoor grill to a direct, medium heat setting, aiming for a temperature between 350°F and 375°F.

For 3 pounds of chicken wings that are still whole, use a chef's knife or kitchen shears to cut through the first joint of each wing, and remove the wing tips.

Discard or freeze the wing tips for stock.

To prepare the wings, first cut through the second joint to separate each wing into two pieces: the flat (forearm) and the drumette (upper arm).

Pat the wings dry using paper towels, then place them into a spacious bowl.

Season with 2 teaspoons of baking powder, 2 teaspoons of cornstarch, and 1 teaspoon of kosher salt.

Mix the wings well to ensure they are evenly coated.

Preheat the grill and clean the grates.

If needed, grill the wings in batches, placing them in a single layer with space between each piece.

Cover the grill and cook, turning every 5 minutes, until the wings are cooked through and the skin is crisp and golden brown, approximately 25 to 30 minutes.

About 10 minutes before the wings are done, prepare the sauce.

Make the sauce:

Mince 2 garlic cloves.
Peel a 1-inch piece of fresh ginger and finely grate it to yield 1 tablespoon.
Melt 2 tablespoons unsalted butter in a small saucepan over medium-low heat.
Add the garlic and ginger until they release their aromatic flavors, cooking for about 1 minute.
Add 1/4 cup honey, 2 tablespoons gochujang, 2 tablespoons soy sauce, 1 tablespoon plus 1 1/2 teaspoon rice vinegar, and 1 teaspoon toasted sesame oil.
Stir the mixture vigorously until everything is well blended, then continue cooking for approximately 30 seconds, or until the mixture is thoroughly heated.
Turn off the heat. (Alternatively, place the butter, garlic, and ginger in a microwave-safe bowl and microwave in 30-second intervals until the butter is melted.)

Once the wings are cooked to perfection, move them to a spacious bowl.
Pour the sauce over them and toss thoroughly to ensure an even coating.
For a finishing touch, sprinkle with thinly sliced scallions and a dash of white sesame seeds if you like.

Chicken Teriyaki

Ingredients

1 tablespoon vegetable or canola oil
1 1/2 pounds boneless, skinless chicken
thighs
1 teaspoon kosher salt
1/3 cup mirin
1/3 cup sake
1/4 cup soy sauce or tamari
1/4 cup water
2 tablespoons of tightly packed light or dark
brown sugar
1 tablespoon cornstarch
1 medium scallion, thinly sliced (optional)
White sesame seeds, for garnish (optional)
Steamed white rice and cooked broccoli, for
serving

How to Make

Add 1 tablespoon of vegetable or canola oil to a large (12-inch) frying pan and heat over medium-high heat until the oil starts to shimmer. Meanwhile, pat 1 1/2 pounds boneless, skinless chicken thighs dry with paper towels and season all over with 1 teaspoon kosher salt.

Arrange the chicken in the pan in a single layer and let it cook undisturbed for 4 to 6 minutes, or until the bottom is nicely browned.

While the chicken cooks, prepare the sauce by combining 1/3 cup mirin, 1/3 cup sake, 1/4 cup soy sauce or tamari, 1/4 cup water, and 2 tablespoons of light or dark brown sugar in a medium bowl.

Whisk the mixture until the sugar is completely dissolved.

Transfer 2 tablespoons of the sauce to a small bowl, add 1 tablespoon corn starch, and whisk until the cornstarch is suspended.

Flip the chicken.

Add the sauce (excluding the cornstarch) to the chicken and bring the mixture to a boil.

Adjust the heat to keep it at a gentle simmer, ensuring it bubbles steadily without boiling too vigorously.

Simmer until the chicken is cooked through, 5 to 10 minutes more.

Reduce the heat to medium.

Using tongs, carefully lift the chicken and place it onto a clean cutting board.

Whisk the cornstarch mixture again.
With continuous whisking, gradually incorporate the cornstarch mixture into the sauce.
Continue cooking, stirring constantly, until the sauce reaches a thickened consistency, which should take about 30 seconds.
Turn off the heat.

Slice the chicken into 1/2-inch strips, arranging them in a large, shallow dish.
Drizzle the sauce evenly over the chicken.
For an extra touch of flavor and presentation, top with finely sliced scallions and a sprinkle of white sesame seeds if you like.
Serve with cooked white rice with cooked broccoli.

Three Cup Chicken Recipe

Ingredients

1 (2-inch) piece ginger
5 cloves garlic
4 medium scallions
1/2 cup Shaoxing wine
1/2 cup soy sauce
1/4 cup water
2 tablespoons packed dark brown sugar
2 tablespoons dark soy sauce
1 tablespoon Chinese black vinegar
2 tablespoons toasted sesame oil, divided
2 1/2 pounds chicken wings, cut into flats and drumettes

1 tablespoon cornstarch
1 tablespoon of neutral oil, like canola or vegetable oil (offers a mild flavor and high smoke point, making it an ideal choice for sautéing, frying, and baking without altering the taste of your dish)
2 dried Sichuan or Chinese chili peppers
1 medium bunch Thai basil
Cooked white rice, for serving

How to Make

Peel 1 (2-inch) piece ginger.
Thinly cut lengthwise into planks.
Stack several planks of ginger and slice them lengthwise into thin,
matchstick-sized strips.
Continue this process until the entire piece of ginger is cut into
slender matchsticks.
Thinly slice 5 garlic cloves.
Trim and cut 4 medium scallions crosswise into 3 pieces each.
Place 1/2 cup Shaoxing wine, 1/2 cup soy sauce, 1/4 cup water, 2
tablespoons packed dark brown sugar, 2 tablespoons dark soy
sauce, 1 tablespoon Chinese black vinegar, and Pour 1 tablespoon
of toasted sesame oil into a liquid measuring cup or a medium-
sized bowl.
Use a whisk to mix the oil until it's well combined.

Pat 2 1/2 pounds of chicken wing flats and drumettes dry with
paper towels, then transfer them to a large bowl. Toss with 1
tablespoon of cornstarch until all pieces are coated.

Heat a large skillet or wok over medium-high heat and add 1
tablespoon of neutral oil.
Arrange the chicken in a single layer in the skillet and cook for
about 4 to 5 minutes on each side, or until the chicken is lightly
browned.
Remove the chicken from the skillet and place it on a plate,
allowing it to rest while you continue with the recipe.

In the same skillet, add the remaining 1 tablespoon of toasted sesame oil (no need to clean the skillet) and let it heat for a few seconds.

Add the ginger, garlic, scallions, and 2 dried Sichuan or Chinese peppers.

Stir-fry until fragrant, 1 to 2 minutes.

Transfer the chicken and any juices from the plate back into the pan.

Pour in the sauce and thoroughly combine by stirring until everything is evenly mixed.

Ensure the chicken pieces are fully immersed in the sauce.

Simmer, stirring occasionally and reducing the heat as needed, until the sauce is reduced by half and coats the chicken, 15 to 20 minutes.

Remove the leaves from one medium bunch of Thai basil, discarding the stems.

Turn off the heat.

Sprinkle the basil leaves over the chicken and toss gently until the leaves begin to wilt and release their aroma.

Serve the chicken and sauce with cooked white rice.

Spicy Labneh Fried Chicken Sandwich

Ingredients

For the chicken:

1 cup labneh
1/4 cup hot sauce, such as Cholula
2 1/4 teaspoons kosher salt, divided
2 teaspoons garlic powder, divided
1 teaspoon freshly ground black pepper, divided
6 tender and juicy boneless, skinless chicken thighs, weighing
between 1 1/2 to 2 pounds
1 cup all-purpose flour
1 teaspoon smoked paprika
1/2 teaspoon cayenne pepper
4 cups vegetable oil, such as canola

For the sandwiches:

1 large ripe mango
1 large ripe avocado
6 brioche buns
6 tablespoons chipotle mayonnaise
6 tablespoons mango chutney
1 1/2 cups of lightly packed baby arugula, weighing approximately 1 1/2 ounces.
18 to 24 dill bread-and-butter pickle chips

How to Make

Make the chicken:

Place 1 cup labneh, 1/4 cup hot sauce, 1 1/2 teaspoons of the kosher salt, 1 teaspoon of the garlic powder, and 1/2 teaspoon of the black pepper in a large bowl and whisk to combine.

Add 6 boneless, skinless chicken thighs to a bowl and toss them until they are well coated.
Cover the bowl and let the chicken marinate in the refrigerator for at least 2 hours, or up to overnight for deeper flavor.
n a shallow bowl or pie plate, combine 1 cup all-purpose flour, 3/4 teaspoon kosher salt, 1 teaspoon garlic powder, 1/2 teaspoon black pepper, 1 teaspoon smoked paprika, and 1/2 teaspoon cayenne pepper.
Mix the ingredients thoroughly until they are uniformly combined.

To bread the chicken, remove each piece from the labneh mixture and dredge it in the flour mixture.
Press the flour mixture onto the chicken to ensure it adheres well and gets into all the crevices.
Arrange the coated chicken pieces on a rimmed baking sheet or large plate in a single layer.

Heat 4 cups of vegetable oil in a Dutch oven or large cast-iron skillet over medium-high heat until it reaches 350°F, ensuring the oil level is about 1 inch up the sides of the pan. While the oil heats, peel, pit, and slice 1 large ripe mango and 1 large avocado very thinly for your sandwiches. Place a wire rack on a baking sheet and preheat your oven to 200°F. Fry the chicken in batches of 2 to 3 pieces: Carefully add the chicken to the hot oil and cook until golden brown and the internal temperature reaches at least 165°F, about 3 to 5 minutes per side. Transfer the chicken to the rack and keep warm in the oven while you fry the remaining chicken.

Assemble the sandwiches:
When ready to assemble, remove the chicken from the oven and heat the oven to broil. Split 6 brioche buns in half and place cut-side up in a single layer on a baking sheet. Broil the buns until they are lightly toasted, which should take about 1 to 2 minutes. On the cut side of each bottom bun, spread 1 tablespoon of chipotle mayo, then place a crispy fried chicken thigh on top. Distribute 1 1/2 cups of baby arugula evenly over the chicken. Layer each sandwich with 4 to 5 slices of fresh mango, followed by an even spread of avocado. Add 3 to 4 pickle chips on each sandwich. Finally, spread 1 tablespoon of mango chutney on the cut side of each top bun and place it, chutney-side down, over the pickles to complete the sandwiches.

Chicken Enchiladas

Ingredients

Cooking spray
1 (15-ounce) can enchilada sauce
1 (4-ounce) can diced green chilis (do not drain)
4 cups shredded, cooked chicken (from a 3 to 4 -pound roasted chicken)
1 (15-ounce) can black beans, drained
3 1/2 cups of shredded Mexican cheese blend, separated into portions
1/4 cup fresh cilantro leaves, finely chopped and separated
8 (10-inch) large flour tortillas

How to Make

Heat the oven and prepare the baking dish.
Place a rack in the center of the oven and preheat it to 400°F.
Lightly coat a 9x13-inch baking dish with non-stick cooking spray to ensure easy release and prevent sticking.
Make the sauce.
Stir the enchilada sauce and the green chilis and their liquid together in a small bowl.
Pour 1 cup of this sauce evenly into the base of the baking dish and set it aside.
Make the filling.
In a medium bowl, combine the chicken, black beans, 2 cups of shredded cheese, 1/2 cup of the enchilada sauce mixture, and 2 tablespoons of cilantro.
Gently toss the ingredients with tongs until the chicken and cheese are evenly coated with the sauce.

Roll the tortillas.
Take one tortilla at a time and place ¾ cup of the filling along the center.
Roll the tortilla snugly around the filling, then place it seam side down in the baking dish.
Fold the ends of each tortilla underneath to seal them.
As you add more filled tortillas to the dish, pack them closely together to form a compact casserole.
Top the enchiladas.
Top the filled enchiladas with the remaining enchilada sauce mixture (you'll have about 3/4 cup).
Top with the remaining 1 1/2 cups of cheese, ensuring an even distribution across the surface.

Bake for 20 minutes or until browned and bubbly.
Bake until the enchilada sauce is bubbling vigorously and the cheese has melted and started to turn golden brown, about 20 to 25 minutes.
Cool for 5 minutes before serving.
Let the enchiladas rest for 5 minutes to cool slightly, then sprinkle the remaining cilantro over the top before serving.

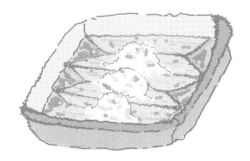

Slow Cooker Chicken Tinga

Ingredients

4 boneless, skinless chicken breasts (about 2 pounds total)

1 teaspoon kosher salt, plus additional salt for seasoning to taste.

Freshly ground black pepper

2 tablespoons olive oil

1 medium yellow onion, thinly sliced

3 cloves garlic, minced

1 teaspoon ground cumin

1/2 teaspoon dried oregano

1 bay leaf

1 (14-ounce) can tomato purée

Add a burst of smoky heat to your dishes with 2 minced canned chipotle peppers in adobo sauce, combined with 1 tablespoon of the rich, tangy sauce.

Serving options:
Corn tortillas
Diced red onion
Avocado
Fresh cilantro

How to Make

Season the chicken generously with salt and pepper.
Arrange the pieces in a single layer inside a 4-quart or larger slow cooker.
In a medium skillet, warm the oil over medium heat until it begins to shimmer and lightly ripple.
Add the onion and cook, stirring occasionally, until it becomes soft, about 5 minutes.
Incorporate the garlic, cumin, oregano, bay leaf, and 1 teaspoon of salt, and mix well.
Stir in the tomato purée, chipotle peppers, and adobo sauce, then bring the mixture to a boil.
Lower the heat and let it simmer for 5 minutes.
Pour the prepared sauce and onions over the chicken in the slow cooker.
Cover and cook until the chicken is thoroughly cooked and tender —2 to 3 hours on the LOW setting or 1 to 2 hours on the HIGH setting.
Once the slow cooker is turned off, carefully transfer the chicken to a clean cutting board. Discard the bay leaf, then use two forks to shred the chicken into bite-sized pieces. Return the shredded chicken to the slow cooker, mixing well to coat it with the sauce.
Serve the chicken in tortillas with your favorite toppings, if desired.

Chicken Strips Recipe

Ingredients

2 boneless, skinless chicken breasts (1 to 1 1/4 pounds)
1/2 cup all-purpose flour
3/4 teaspoon kosher salt, divided
2 teaspoons garlic powder, divided
2 teaspoons Italian seasoning, divided
2 large eggs
1 1/2 cups panko bread crumbs
1/4 cup white sesame seeds (optional)
Vegetable oil, for frying

How to Make

Cut the skinless, boneless chicken breasts into strips by slicing across the grain, aiming for pieces that are approximately 1 inch wide and 2 inches long.

Place 1/2 cup all-purpose flour, 1 teaspoon of the garlic powder, 1 teaspoon of the Italian seasoning, and 1/4 teaspoon of the kosher salt in a wide, shallow bowl, and whisk to combine. Place 2 large eggs and 1/4 teaspoon of the kosher salt in second shallow bowl and whisk until well combined. Place 1 1/2 cups panko bread crumbs, 1/4 cup white sesame seeds if using, the remaining 1 teaspoon garlic powder, 1 teaspoon Italian seasoning, and 1/4 teaspoon kosher salt in In a separate bowl, add the ingredients and use a whisk to thoroughly mix them together.

Working in batches of 3 to 4 strips, first coat the chicken in flour, shaking off any excess. Next, dip each strip into beaten egg, letting any excess egg drip off by swiping it against the bowl's edge. Then, roll the chicken strips in bread crumbs, ensuring they are evenly coated. Arrange the coated strips on a baking sheet or large plate and let them rest for 10 minutes to allow the coating to adhere properly.

Preheat a large skillet with enough vegetable oil to cover the bottom by about 1/8 inch (approximately 1 cup for a 10-inch skillet) over medium heat until it reaches 350°F. To test if the oil is ready, drop a small piece of panko into the oil; it should sizzle immediately and take a minute to turn golden brown. Working in 2 to 3 batches, add the breaded chicken strips to the hot oil and fry until they are crisp and golden brown, about 3 minutes per side. Transfer the cooked chicken to a wire rack set over a rimmed baking sheet to drain excess oil.

Made in United States
Orlando, FL
28 March 2025

59931920R00031